Wisdom from the Mind of a Young Man

By: Kendrick Bailey

Cover designed by Keywon Jackson

Photography by Keywon Jackson

Edited by Kathy Hardison

Edited by LaToyia Jackson

ISBN-10:

0986266027

ISBN-13:

978-0-9862660-2-7

Copyright © 2014 - Kendrick Bailey

All Rights Reserved.

Dedicated to my loving, kind, understanding and wise mother, Rhonda Brown, who never gave up on me. Thanks for all the calm talks and passionately heated debates which have taught me so much.

I love you dearly, Mom!

Acknowledgments

First, I would like to thank Almighty God, for without Him none of these thoughts could have been conceived and let alone come to life. Secondly, I would like to thank, Rhonda and Arelexus Brown for giving me a peaceful environment to work in and for their support, undivided attention, honest opinions, and just a listening ear. I also would like to thank my financial friend, who saw a need and planted a seed. You know who you are! I greatly appreciate, Mrs. Kathy Hardison and Mrs. LaToyia Jackson, who dedicated their time and energy to edit and proofread my book! Lastly I would like to thank my true and faithful friend, Keywon Jackson, who pulled all-nighters with me, gave his honest opinion, lent a listening ear, and helped my vision come to life!

I greatly appreciate all of you!!!

Preface

Wisdom from the Mind of a Young Man started solely as a book of quotes. Just five months prior, I underwent a major spinal surgery due to Scoliosis. I was not able to bend, lift anything over five or ten pounds, twist, or squat for six months. I was confined to my rolling computer chair and the round kitchen table.

I was taking the strongest pain medications that were prescribed for my medical needs and I felt that I was getting dumber by the day. I decided to do a lot of reading, which mostly was in vain because I could not comprehend what I was reading. After three months I had enough; I took myself off of the meds cold turkey.

About a month later, I decided I would try to clear the thick fog that had loomed over my brain by trying to recall my life lessons and values that were instilled in me as a child by my mother, thus deciding to write a quote book. Except for the "roses are red" type of poems, I had never written a poem in my 22 years. The very first one came to me while gazing at the stars in the park. Having no pen or pad at the time, I typed it in my phone as a draft text message.

After reading it to my mom and sister and earning praise, the poems started flooding in from then on. However, they would come at the most inconvenient times, such as when I'm almost asleep. I would then have to make the choice of a lifetime, either go to sleep or wake up and write the poem. Laziness and technology were my friends during these nights. I would sluggishly roll over grab my phone and type the poem as a draft text message. With the help of a lot of meditation, observation of nature, and reflection of the world we live in, the book was completed within three months. I sincerely hope you enjoy reading it as much as I enjoyed writing it! It is my greatest wish that you will gain insight and wisdom as you flip throughout the pages.

Wisdom from the Mind of a Young Man is a reflection book. These thoughts, quotes, and poems should not just be read, but reflected upon if you truly seek to gain the wisdom within the following pages. With these keys, unlock the *Wisdom from the Mind of a Young Man*.

Table of Contents

Quotes

- Wisdom of the World
- Courage to Be Feared
- The Life You Lead
- Ticking of Time
- Sovereignty
- Reflecting upon Reflection

Poems

- Stars
- The Looking Glass
- Empty Dreams
- Lover's Letter
- Loss of Innocence
- Tomorrow
- Bounded by Beauty
- Trapped in the Mirror
- A Woman's Praise
- The Sovereign
- The Surreptitious Serpent
- Sea of Despair
- Empty but Full
- The Sinner's Salvation
- Age of Ambition
- Perfectly Imperfect
- What Is It Truly To Be a Man?
- Perception, Deception, or Misconception?
- From Darkness to Light
- Help Me to Remember

Wisdom of the World

🪨 In a world full of distractions, it is easy to lose focus of what is important. I would urge you to discern what is of real value.

🪨 If we could learn to set aside our differences and embrace each other with love... Just imagine!

🪨 Never do anything halfheartedly, for it could be wholly responsible for your advancement.

🪨 Sometimes to win is to lose, and to lose is to win.

🪨 If you survive the suffering, you will find a sense of satisfaction.

- No one ever thought he would fall until he did.

- Licks from a fist can heal quickly; one lick from the tongue can take a lifetime to heal.

- When you learn from other's mistakes, that's one less rocky road you have to take.

- When I am high I can be low, and when I am low I can be high.

- Fall back from foolishness and you will find a sense of freedom.

- Laziness and lack live on the same land.

- The sun shines the brightest after the storm has passed.

- Usually a know-it-all knows nothing at all.

- People can be like leeches. They will suck you dry and move on to the next victim, so be careful whom you give yourself to.

- Two eyes, two ears, one mouth.

- Once words exit one's mouth, they can never be taken back.

- No one is insignificant; we each possess wonderful characteristics, gifts, and talents.

- When you have doubt, your dreams are doomed; when you have faith, your dreams will bloom.

- Everyone seeks acceptance.

- Learn to appreciate what you have instead of complaining about what you do not have.

- The road to success is a long, tiring journey with many obstacles. You must be well-winded, strong-willed, and wise in order to withstand.

- Two things that everyone has in common are love and laughter.

- Even the dimmest star shines bright when the time is right.

- To the heart, a word of encouragement is a seed of nourishment.

- Forgiveness brings forth freedom.

- In the eyes of a child, a parent can do no wrong.

- Everyone desires to be loved, and when it is not given, it is found in fraudulent faces and places.

🪨 What you see is generally not what it seems to be.

🪨 If you knew the food you were being served was poisonous, you would not eat it. So, why do we continue to feed our mind, body, and soul the poison being offered to us on a daily basis?

🪨 The truth is everyone has suffered, will suffer, or is suffering."

🪨 A true leader leads by example.

🪨 A winner never looked like a winner until he won, so who's to say you aren't one?

- You have reached a level of maturity when seeing others win makes you feel as if you have won.

- As a river constantly flows downstream, so should you, bursting forth with tenacity, moving or overcoming every obstacle in the way, until you reach the ocean of opportunity.

- Sometimes a simple smile can make the difference in someone's day.

- We are headed for troubled times; there has been a compromise of moral standards. Everyone is seeking self-gratification, only to gain what they will lose.

- A mother is to be the example of the type of woman her daughter should become and the type of woman her son should seek.

- Just because you are wandering doesn't mean you are lost, and just because you are lost doesn't mean you can't be found.

- Whatever you are pursuing with persistence and perseverance shall proceed to provide satisfaction once it submits.

- A snake is a snake; it may shed its skin but it will still be a snake.

🌿 Your words can bring life or death.

🌿 Where love lives, you can usually find life on the same street.

🌿 Man, treat your woman like the queen she is; woman, treat your man like the king he is.

🌿 Like a deep-rooted, tall-standing tree is how a man should strive to be, providing love, comfort, and shelter to all those who confide in him, while being able to withstand the storms of life without falling or failing those who depend on him.

Courage to Be Feared

- Fear is a false illusion; face it and it will flee.

- Fail until you fight; fight until you fail; but the only way you truly fail is when you bail.

- When you finally decide to take a stand, you will realize that the entire time the power was in your hand.

- Fear has never formed anything great; fear has only forgone failure until it was faced.

- Fear is a false reality that keeps us from moving forward.

We all have the courage to conquer, but first we must cut off the cowardly counterparts contained within us causing us to conform to continuous containment.

The Life You Lead

🐾 Take time to invest in people, for when you do, you bring out the best in them.

🐾 Preparation provides proliferation.

🐾 It is rare that you find someone who genuinely cares about you; but if you do happen to, cherish them.

🐾 What good is a dream that in order to gain you must scheme?

🐾 Following forgoes the fall.

🐾 When you create monsters, they will come back to find you.

🪨 Do not do what you want to do; do what is right to do.

🪨 People or possessions, which will you have? If you lose possessions, you can get them back. If you lose people, well I'm afraid you will not get them back.

🪨 In all you do, be sincere.

🪨 The future is foretold from today.

🪨 Sometimes humility hurts, but in the end you will see its worth.

🪨 Shady schemes bring tears in streams.

🐾 Think with precision before you make a decision.

🐾 Take time to slow down and look around; the world we live in is so profound.

🐾 Be thankful for what is done for you; no one owes you anything.

🐾 Do not purposely lead people astray, for in the end, you will surely have your day.

🐾 Cruelty can lead to casualties and catastrophe.

🐾 Just because you are going through something doesn't give you the right to treat others cruelly; they may be going through something as well.

- Life is like a roller-coaster, strap up, hold on tight, and enjoy the ride.

- At the end of pain, there is usually a gain, as long as you don't allow yourself to stay linked to the chain.

- Take off the mask, remove the disguise; for if it is truth you despise, you will meet your demise.

- When you try to change others, you usually lose yourself along the way.

- Idle words and empty promises lead to broken hearts.

🪨 Things have to have order; your life has to have structure; you cannot just live any way you want to.

🪨 Just because you're high enough to look down doesn't mean when I look up I should be astounded.

🪨 When you go places your character cannot keep you, you will be sure to join those who you thought were once beneath you.

🪨 When people include you in their life, it is a gift that is given, not an entitlement.

🪨 Just because the word "friend" has the word "end" in it doesn't mean they will be there to the end, for most generally wish to see you come to an end.

- Cherish people, for they are here today and could be gone tomorrow.

- Lies lived lead to loss of life.

- Fakes and snakes come with gifts and baits, only to take your place and erase your space.

- To build yourself up and tear others down will leave you standing with only rubble and no one around.

- Saying you're only going to do it once is like sticking your toe in the water; the next thing you know, you're fully submerged.

- I have no problem with failure because I know the more I fail the closer I get to success.

- Rectify problems while they're small because when you don't, they cause even the greatest of men to fall.

- Have humility. You are better than no one.

- A legacy is the only thing that can be left once you take your last breath.

The Ticking of Time

🪨 Time and life are two nonrefundable gifts.

🪨 Life passes by quickly. The more you rush through it, the sooner it will end.

🪨 Your words and thoughts will determine your life tomorrow.

🪨 Seize the seasons for they come and go.

🪨 Your destiny is waiting to meet you; start moving towards it.

🪨 Change your ways while you have time, for you never know when it may be your time.

🪨 Time is one of the most valuable treasures wasted daily.

Sovereignty

✦ Serenity and peace come from heaven... just look to the sky.

✦ Living for Christ, you live twice and die once; living for the world, you live once and die twice.

✦ Nothing is done in our own strength; the Lord is always behind the scenes.

✦ Sometimes the Lord uses people as sandpaper to smooth down our rough spots.

✦ Pursue God and blessings will pursue you.

✦ If you go through hell on earth, what sense does it make to go to hell once you leave the earth?

🪨 Guidance and grace are gifts from God.

🪨 We should not pray to get, but instead pray to give.

🪨 Prayer leads to presence, and presence leads to peace.

🪨 Your story doesn't have to be where God delivered you from. It can be where God delivered you to by doing what's right.

🪨 Some things are inexplicable; you just have to know that there is a higher power out there that is more mighty and mind-boggling than anyone could ever imagine.

🕊 With God at the head, you can't help but to get ahead.

🕊 From the womb, we are born into wickedness; whether we realize and submit will determine if we are reborn into righteousness.

Reflecting

upon

Reflection

🐾 Everyone possesses a key; it is key to find out what it unlocks.

🐾 Even the wise once had foolish ways.

🐾 You can learn something from anything if you take the time to reflect upon it.

🐾 As quickly as it comes is as quickly as it goes.

🐾 You only live once if you live like a dunce.

🪨 You must be willing to sacrifice something in order to gain anything, but you should first decide whether what you are sacrificing will be worth what you could possibly lose.

🪨 Nothing can come from something, but something can't come from nothing.

🪨 Wisdom is like a gold nugget. It comes in many shapes and sizes. Some are worth more than others, and anyone who searches in the right place can find it, but it is what you do with it that determines its true worth.

🐍 Scars are a sign of strength; they are there to show the world you went through something and survived.

🐍 As beauties embrace, humans deface.

🐍 There comes a time when one must evaluate the true meaning of love.

🐍 Is the seed more important than the tree, and the tree more important than the fruit it bears?

🐍 In this wooded world, always expect a snake.

- In one's moments of desperation comes their greatest inspiration.

- Where wisdom can be seen, foolishness can be keen.

- Temptation is not what's around you, it's what's in you.

- Just because it has no sound does not mean it cannot be profound.

- Along with desire comes the opportunity for deceit.

- If you fear to fail, then you will fail to fear.

🪨 The most important things are under the surface.

🪨 Simple but sound is the trail of ants going to and from the mound.

🪨 Constant contemplation will eventually result in being complacent.

🪨 Wisdom and wealth come to those who constantly seek it, but poverty and procrastination come to those who only speak it.

🪨 The best thing about a bad day is it doesn't last forever. It has to end.

- Anything you demand with determination and wise decisions will be delivered.

- The mother of change is the ability to envision a better future.

- We are all trapped in our thoughts. They can either be the key that locks or unlocks the cell.

- Every rich person is poor in a sense; every poor person is rich in a sense.

- Every bad person is good in a sense; every good person is bad in a sense.

🪨 A rock through the formation of other rocks became a boulder.

🪨 Evil speaks louder than good, but it is the soft spoken voices that should be heard and understood.

🪨 Silence is something you should seek, for when you do, the Almighty will speak.

🪨 Ignorance is costly; if you take the time to assess the value of what's in your hand, you can make an opportunity out of what may have once seemed to be valueless.

🪨 The beginning of anything begins in the heart, transfers to the head, and comes to life through the hands.

🪨 Remember, everything burns. The only thing you have the opportunity to fireproof is your soul.

🪨 Taking time for reflection is sure to give you a new sense of direction.

🪨 With constant effort, could not the small ax chop down the huge oak tree?

🪨 Sometimes a warning will come as a whisper, and deception's voice will sound a lot crisper.

🪨 Comfort and complacency are unconstitutional.

🕭 As fall comes before winter and spring comes before summer, so should a man expect rain when he hears thunder.

🕭 I will only fear death when I fear that I will not find eternal life after falling from death.

🕭 You never have a bad day; you only have a bad moment in a day. If you decide to let that moment determine your day, then it will surely become a bad day.

🕭 Something as sweet as a kiss can come before a betrayal.

🕭 If you live long enough, you will see the student become the teacher, and the teacher become the student.

- Conscious compromise leads to one's demise.

- The will to do good lives in all of us. It is just the constant presence of the temptation to do evil that persuades us to partake in it.

- Everyone has been given the gift of influence, but only you can decide whether you will be a positive or negative influence in someone's life.

- At the top of the mountain, you will see all the paths that you could have taken to get there a lot quicker, but you will be satisfied because although the path you took may have taken you a lot longer, the journey will have made you a lot stronger.

<u>Poems</u>

Poems

Stars

Stars, stars, O' marvelous stars!

How I wish, I wish I could visit you where you are.

You give us the privilege to gaze at you from afar.

You shine bold and bright even on the dimmest night,

cannot be compared to even the brightest light,

cannot be held behind a set of bars, nor put on a shelf in a measly jar.

O' if you could sing it'd be heavenly bars,

 and you'd tell glorious stories of Venus, Pluto, Jupiter and Mars.

Stars, stars O' marvelous stars! No matter how wonderful I may think you are,

my Heavenly Father says I'm more important than you by far.

The Looking Glass

When you look through the looking glass, what do you see?

The person you are or wish to be?

A need for love or love to give?

A troubled life or life to live?

The hand to take or heart to give?

Is it materialistic, or simply simplistic?

Could it be a dreamer, or maybe a schemer?

Do you speak blunt, or is it a front?

A beautiful girl caught in the tricks of the world?

Or a shy guy who just wants to be fly?

Do you take it and run, or stay and ask why?

Do you hold it inside, or break down and cry?

Are you lost on your way, or on your way to be lost?

Do you think there's no hope?

Or know someone who was hung on a cross not a rope?

Empty Dreams

You're chasing the wind my friend,

evading life and living in sin,

looking to fill a hole,

pursuing empty dreams, willing to lose your soul.

You have to give God control.

If He's not the head, it takes a toll.

Your actions are brash and bold,

but deep in your heart, you feel so cold.

You've searched faces and places

only to find empty spaces.

So now, look to Jesus, for it's sin He erases.

It's not in a drug or even a club.

So put down the shovel. It's your grave you dug,

for there is a serpent and also a dove.

But if you want true life, seek the One above.

Lover's Letter

Love, love, love is what I seek.

But I keep it deep inside because it's something I dare not speak.

To be held and to hold, to love deep and grow old.

To have grandchildren around with stories being told.

Is it a fictional fantasy to far from my grasp?

To have the love of my life is all that I ask.

 To bring joy everyday would be my life's task.

With kisses and kindness I'd keep her heart warm

and stick by her side through all of life's storms.

Compassion and care would come from these arms

followed by two firm fists to keep my baby from harm.

Protection, provision is what I would be,

to know she only puts God before me.

Can't wait for the day I get down on one knee to ask the woman of my dreams, My wife will you be?

Loss of Innocence

When innocence is lost so is morality.

It brings pureness to death and life to fatality.

It's not flesh and blood but spiritual principalities.

So when I see women half dressed, how can I go about it casually?

Seeing men be seduced to sexual sin

 is like Eve passing Adam that fruit once again.

But men must resist the seductress's kiss,

or surely we'll fall into the abyss.

Woman, do not be deceived by mere talks of bliss,

or your man of God you'll probably miss.

Your body has value much more than you know.

It's not to be used to take you where you'd like to go.

You'll get there in time; just trust in the Lord.

You're the daughter of the King, so you should be adored

because a Proverbs 31 woman simply can't be ignored.

Tomorrow

Tomorrow can give; tomorrow can take.

It can leave you lifeless or allow you to wake.

For it can be small or it can be great.

It can allow you to love, forbid you to hate.

It may bring you joy or it may bring you sorrow,

but be thankful for today because you may not see tomorrow.

Bounded by Beauty

Her lips spoke of love, but also of lies.

Her body smelled sweet, yet was surrounded with flies.

I thought it was life, but there was death in her eyes,

and whispers of fallen men came from between her thighs.

Her tongue tasted of taffy, entangled in trust.

Though lips overlaid and were layered with lust.

Her breast perfectly rounded with persuasion and precision

could make even a man of the clearest thought make a rash decision.

Her skin soft as silk seduced me to sin,

and her perfectly sculpted body made me do it again.

Her hair, O' so heavenly, how it blew in the wind

And how she loved to whistle that tune "You Can't Win."[1]

For me she was no good, so it came to an end.

But here I find her lying in my arms once again.

---

[1] "You Can't Win" – Michael Jackson

Trapped in the Mirror

Trapped in the mirror she checks every ten minutes.

Not knowing what she's been told was beauty was a lie and a gimmick--

Told if she dresses this way, she'll get all the guys,

but not told what she'll attract is a man full of lies.

Told that her body and looks are her only real assets,

but not knowing that her true worth exceeds way past that.

She's been led down a path that was laid down with lies--

Told to lay on her back, and then she will rise,

but those are straight lies and words I despise.

True beauty is good character that will bring confidence to the carrier,

along with the study of her Bible and books, she will break through any barrier.

A Woman's Praise

To be praised by a woman is what a man longs to hear.

For words to drip from her lips sweet as honey saying, "You can do it dear."

To hear her say, "I believe in you." Simple but philosophical,

although to the world, what he's trying to do may seem impossible.

To hear words that encourage, rather than words that discourage

will make even the smallest of men stand bold full of courage.

The Sovereign

When you soak in the silence, the Sovereign will speak.

He gives grace to those who graciously follow His feet.

He sends forth a victorious victory to those facing defeat,

and His Holy hands will uphold the humble and meek.

He gives strength to those who feel O' so helpless and weak

and a voice to those who the world would say shouldn't speak.

So if you are any of those things, the Sovereign is someone whom

 I would suggest you seek.

The Surreptitious Serpent

The surreptitious serpent slithers and slides,

secretly serenading men's ears with straight lies

telling us, "Why walk when you know you can fly?"

Saying, "Do it this once, just give it a try."

You only live once, but sure that's a lie

because if you live right, you'll live when you die.

"Do what thou wilt" is what they will sell you.

But, your soul it will cost is what they don't tell you.

But I know a Savior who's ready to bail you

from the hands of the enemy who's ready to jail you.

Yes, times will get rough and things will be tough,

but trust in God because when He said,

"I will not, will not, will not fail you," it wasn't a bluff.

Sea of Despair

Lost out at sea, drowned in despair.

Living my life, not giving a care.

Ignoring all signs that say swimmers beware.

But it looked like so much fun, for me not to join just wouldn't be fair.

Yes I saw the boundary,

 but on that day I decided to put aside all boundaries that confound me.

The time of my life is where I was headed.

A voice said, "Turn back now." I told him, "Forget it."

What were once screams of joy turned to cries for help.

A sharp pain in my legs is what I suddenly felt.

The courage I gained, it started to melt.

My heart, I recall, was beating so fast,

and water turned from blue to red in a flash.

Those beaded black eyes, O' how they did glow.

Then under the water I surely did go.

Empty but Full

Empty but full, full but empty.

Trying to resist that with which the wicked one would tempt me.

Vices constantly consuming its victims.

What I thought was once real, now I see is just fiction.

Pursuing pleasures that previously seemed priceless

have left me surrounded with things that are worthless and lifeless.

Living to lose, but losing to live.

Feeling forced to take, but forgetting to give.

O' what a waste of this life I have lived.

So what I have left, I guess I will give.

The Sinner's Salvation

Surrounded and seeing no source of escape

until I saw a man in a robe drenched in blood he was draped.

His holy hands had a hole, and his feet they did too.

I said with a stutter, "What, what happened to you?"

He said, "I was sacrificed for the sinner's salvation,

and the blood of the Lamb still suffices the nations."

I said, "Where have you been? I have seen many struggles."

"But you got through them all, so that shows that I love you."

I said, "How can you love me? Have we met before?"

He said, "I gave you a destiny way before you were born,

formed you with my hands and gave you my breath,

then hung on that cross until I had none of it left."

"Then, how are you here?" I exclaimed in great fear.

He said, "I rose from the dead, but son have no fear.

I took the keys to hell and the grave, and their end is near."

I stared at him dazed and said, "Wow you're some guy!"

He said, "I am the One the Only true living God.

At the right hand of the Father I sit in the sky."

I said, "If you are the Son, then who is the Father?"

He said with a smile, "So many questions my son,

but I will simply tell you We are three in one.

For He's God the Father whose will that I do,

and I'm Jesus, His Son. He sent me to you.

Then there's the Holy Spirit who lives in you too."

I fell to the dirt and said, "God I'm a sinner and simply unworthy.

I have run with the devil and my deeds have been dirty."

But He picked me up gently and started to clean.

He said, "For you are my son, your slate I have cleaned.

Now a beacon of hope and light you shall beam."

Age of Ambition

He who doesn't feel pain has been through the flame.

Thoughts of riches run wild in my brain.

It would drive you insane, but I learned to maintain

because I'm simply not satisfied with being stuck in this game.

See, I've tried to count sheep to get me some sleep,

but being slothful and slumbering is success's main thief.

A new form of slavery, that's all that I see,

and crabs in a bucket, that's what surrounds me.

They're serving pollution on a big silver platter.

But before the pig gets slaughtered, it has to get fatter.

See, I covered my eyes and covered my ears,

so I guess that's why my thinking is clear.

A race full of fools since she spoke with the snake.

She offered the fruit, and really you ate?

We could sit and debate on the course you should take,

but time is one thing that refuses to wait.

Perfectly Imperfect

We are loved by a gracious God; yet continue to hoard hate,

told we can do anything, yet we fail to be great.

We are told to forgive, but with cold hearts we live.

We're forgiven again but continue to sin,

told to live at peace, yet find no peace until our enemy's deceased,

saved by God from being consumed by the beast, yet on a daily basis with the devil we feast.

Our ways we should change, I'll say that's the least,

and forgiveness is not given by asking the priest.

There are snakes in the sanctuary that slithered in from the sand,

and doubters and Pharisees that won't see the Promised Land

because the example was set by the One with a hole in each hand.

They tangle the truth and tickle your ears,

when what they should really be telling you is that the end is near.

The Armor of God, you can't buy on TV,

and how I can pay for my sins, well that really beats me

because the last time I checked my salvation was free.

See, I buckled my pants with the Belt of the Truth,

and the Gospel of Peace is the name of my shoe.

The Breastplate of Righteousness covers my chest,

and the Shield of Faith will surely handle the rest.

The Helmet of Salvation is definitely a necessity,

along with the Sword of the Spirit so they can't get the best of me.

You see, it's not about religion, but instead about relationship.

So, seek to be so close to Jesus that you seem tied at the hip.

These rules and regulations they've created are really obsolete.

and I'll never be perfect, but Jesus makes me complete.

So the stones in our hands, we should drop at our feet,

because the only one who can judge us is sitting at the right hand seat.

What Is It Truly To Be a Man?

What is it truly to be a man?

One thing I know for sure, it's to take a stand.

It's not about power or working long hours,

or even coming home with a hand full of flowers.

It's about guidance and kindness,

awakening their eyes that are covered in blindness.

It's not all about who's the bigger man,

but about who can pick up a stranger by reaching out his hand.

He should be the provider and protector, especially of his sector,

but also be gentle with his woman, who to him is as sweet as nectar.

He should raise his children with the righteousness to rule,

but also teach them to steer clear of a fool.

His words should be wise and anger despised.

His tongue should speak truth and never of lies.

Eyes and ears should stay open, observing the scene.

His heart should be pure and his mind should be clean,

knowing that envy's encampment is in the heart of a man

and will take him down quickly, just as sinking sand.

He should know what to do with the power in his hand,

but also remember that he's just a man.

So what is it truly to be a man?

It's to bow down to God and to submit to His plan.

Perception, Deception, or Misconception?

Could it be that what you see as perception is really deception,

and what you've been taught all your life is really a big misconception?

See, when you look at life, it's really perplexed,

but they keep you distracted by asking what's next.

It seems like a hex, how we're stuck in the game

and what we all want seems to be the same.

Building their pyramids without a whip or a chain,

the only way to break free is to first free your brain,

for then you will find clarity in the midst of calamity,

and those who aren't free will claim it's insanity.

Being taught to conform has left us deformed,

and we've been given a false sense of freedom so we'll be disarmed.

But don't be alarmed because you've been forewarned.

Civil liberties broken every day that on the Bible were sworn,

they'll come like a swarm,

bringing to many harm.

There's clues in the music, movies, and more.

They've been trying to tell you what they have in store,

but no one believes it because they've heard it before.

You'll look for the Word, not to find a Bible in sight,

so hide it in your heart, for then you can fight.

For first there was darkness, and then there was light,

but when that light shines, it shines O' so bright.

From Darkness to Light

As I walked through the darkness, I saw a great light,

something like I've never seen, such a marvelous sight.

Couldn't see much around me only sickness and pain,

and the violence and loneliness that had driven me insane.

See, I was born into slavery,

told that I was hopeless from birth and that no one could save me.

Now, as I walked through this valley of the shadow of death,

I can't lie to you, and I can't lie to myself.

See, Fear formed a friendship and Anger an alliance

told me, "Don't go to that light," but I was tired of compliance.

So I took that first step, and I fell on my face.

Fear said, "I told you, my friend, now stay in your place."

But I got back up and said, "I'll try it again!"

Took two steps forward, looked back, and Fear was gone with the wind.

So as I traveled and tried to find my way to this light,

I kept hearing voices say, "Go left. No go right."

But I listened to the still small voice that said, "Keep straight, my son."

And as I got closer, that light shone like the Son.

When I finally reached that light, the chains fell from my wrists.

Death let go of me, and with Life I was kissed.

Help Me to Remember

Lord, help me to bear my cross

in the times that I'm found and the times that I'm lost,

when I think I should speak but I know it will cost,

when friends turn to foes and foes turn to friends,

when I'm surrounded by vultures patiently awaiting my end.

When I'm caught up in the lust and the lies of the land,

help me to remember that's why You now have a hole in each hand.

When I'm weary and weak and feel I can't stand,

help me to remember that You told me that You have a plan.

When greed plants a seed and says, "Take more than you need,"

help me to remember the thousands with two fish and five loaves You did feed.

When I'm facing the giants, and have no alliance,

help me to remember that it's in You I should put my reliance.

When my old ways come back and try to invade,

help me to remember that the price was already paid.

When sickness and struggle try to strangle my faith,

help me to remember like Job said, "You give it and take it away."

When I struggle and strive, and it's hard to survive,

help me remember You had fresh manna to fall from the sky.

When I don't know the answers and question You why,

help me to remember that You catch every tear that I cry.

And finally, when death is at my door and my life is no more,

help me to remember that it's You I lived for, so my life is eternal and I'll see death no more.

For more quotes, poetry and deep thoughts you can find Kendrick on YouTube and Facebook.

www.youtube.com/wisdomfromthemind

www.facebook.com/wisdomfromthemind

www.ingramcontent.com/pod-product-compliance
Lightning Source LLC
Chambersburg PA
CBHW031203160426
43193CB00008B/483